The Phoenix Livin

<hr />

HAND IN HAND

*For Jenny Lea
with best wishes
from
Jon Stallworthy*

Poets Published in
The Phoenix Living Poets Series
★
JAMES AITCHISON
ALEXANDER BAIRD · ALAN BOLD
R. H. BOWDEN · FREDERICK BROADIE
GEORGE MACKAY BROWN · MICHAEL BURN
PHILIP CALLOW · HAYDEN CARRUTH
JOHN COTTON · JENNIFER COUROUCLI
GLORIA EVANS DAVIES
PATRIC DICKINSON
TOM EARLEY · D. J. ENRIGHT
IRENE FEKETE
JOHN FULLER · DAVID GILL
PETER GRUFFYDD
J. C. HALL · MOLLY HOLDEN
JOHN HORDER · P. J. KAVANAGH
RICHARD KELL · LAURIE LEE
LAURENCE LERNER
CHRISTOPHER LEVENSON
EDWARD LOWBURY · NORMAN MACCAIG
ROY McFADDEN
JON MANCHIP WHITE
DIANA McLOGHLEN
JAMES MERRILL · RUTH MILLER
LESLIE NORRIS · ROBERT PACK
RODNEY PYBUS · ARNOLD RATTENBURY
ADRIENNE RICH · ANNE SEXTON · JON SILKIN
JON STALLWORTHY
GILLIAN STONEHAM
EDWARD STOREY · TERENCE TILLER
SYDNEY TREMAYNE
LOTTE ZURNDORFER

HAND IN HAND

by

JON STALLWORTHY

They hand in hand with wandering steps and slow,
Through Eden took their solitary way.

John Milton, *Paradise Lost*

CHATTO AND WINDUS

THE HOGARTH PRESS

1974

Published by
Chatto and Windus Ltd
with The Hogarth Press Ltd
42 William IV Street
London W.C.2

ISBN 7011 2080 2

© Jon Stallworthy 1974

Printed in Great Britain by
Lewis Reprints Ltd.,
The Brown Knight & Truscott Group
London and Tonbridge.

ACKNOWLEDGEMENTS

Acknowledgements are due to the editors of the following anthologies and periodicals in which some of these poems first appeared: *Agenda, Ariel, British Poetry 1972*, edited by Vern Rutsala, *Counter/Measures* (U.S.A.), *The Critical Quarterly, Form, Men and Women*, edited by Louis Untermeyer, *New Humanist, New Statesman, Outposts, PEN New Poetry 1972, Pentametre, Anthology, Samphire, Thirteen Poets*, edited by Dannie Abse for the Poetry Book Society, and *The Times Literary Supplement*.

The sequence *Positives* and the poem 'A Dinner of Herbs' were published as limited editions by the Dolmen Press, Dublin, and the Rougemont Press, Exeter, respectively.

Like all the best recipes, that on page 22 is not original, but my attempts to trace its sources have proved unsuccessful, so I cannot make the grateful acknowledgement I would wish.

CONTENTS

A BOTTLE OF INK

a black thread
reaching from here
to God knows where,
a thread to be broken
every black inch
of its blind way
into the labyrinth.
Tonight I have written
letters that say

I love you and
These days my
poems die
under my hand . . .

Signing my name
I wonder what
sentences lie
coiled in that squat
bottle from which those came,
and why we pay
out lines like this
knowing there is
no going back.

ELEGY FOR A MIS-SPENT YOUTH

Now that the chestnut candles burn
for your birthday, thickening the air
with vapoured sap, my thoughts return
to the attic over the square,
the table with its open book
and a bottle in which the red
sun set, your dress over the back
of a chair, and the bed
where, nightly, drowsy with the fair
exchange of love and with the smell
of chestnut wicks lighting the square,
we never lay and never shall.

TO WHOM IT MAY CONCERN

Cast up
with my
spirited
friend, I
assisted him
off with his
cap. Citizen
Smirnoff, I said,
Tell me about yourself.
He opened his heart to me,
outpouring silence distilled
all those years on the shelf
into philosophy, into poetry,
concluding: You have fulfilled
my destiny. Comrade, I said,
will you fulfil mine? Gladly.
He lets me give him a light,
smokes in silence as I write:
Love, come up and see me here.
Love, my label says DRINK ME.
Love, 1935 was a vintage year.
Snuffing his candle I return
his cap, and watch him start
unsteadily out of the room,
with a message over his heart
for whom it may concern.

WORDS ON A PAPER TABLECLOTH

Tonight, seen through plate-glass
in a café beside the Seine,
the street is a water-colour.
Under the brush of the rain
umbrella after umbrella
grows to full size. They pass

and diminish, half moons,
through all the phases of eclipse
into a streetlamp's nimbus. There
one stops while lovers join lips,
regardless of the street's bright stare.
The rain is strumming tunes

on the sky they stand
under, a star whose horizon
sings. Their music seals them as tight
as our silence when they move on . . .
into the dark . . . into the light . . .
into the dark beyond . . .

WALKING AGAINST THE WIND

'Roast chestnuts, a shilling
a bag.' Shilling and bag
change hands by brazier light.
And there they stand shelling
plump kernels to plug
each other's mouth as tight

as with a kiss. She wears
his blue coat, but the wind
cannot touch him with that
hot nut in his hand
and her thawing fingers
moving towards his mouth.

They shelter in my mind
at midnight, as the brilliant
mosaic towers black out.
Walking against the wind
I wish them a blue coat
for coverlet; jubilant

knowledge of each other;
ignorance that it blows
nowhere on earth so cold
as nightly between those
whom God hath joined together
to have and not to hold.

POSITIVES

1

Black window opposite
bright wall, a head and a lamp between,
a head as full of the night —
and no stars to be seen —
as the lamp is full of its light.

Through glass and a membrane
once painted with your miniature
the dark stares at the dark. The rain
spits at the glass. Is it dark with you,
dear face I may not see again?

All that we left unsaid,
undone, a swarm of bitter negatives,
tonight seethes in my head.
Nothing of our love lives —
the children you wanted

lie locked in my scrotum —
till I turn to the lamp-lit sheet,
and the pen stirs under my thumb
as your breast stirred under it,
and the words come.

2

       Saying 'I love you'
and hearing 'I love you' spoken,
the last seal on the lips broken
       by a foreign tongue,

       I am not I; and who
are you; and why did our verb not
ever before mean this; and what
       now is its meaning?

       Dearest, if we knew
tonight more than the gods allow,
hearing their sentence, should we now
       stand as we do?

15

3

They noticed together
how the mirror held them
as they held each other,
locked in an oval frame.

Such luminous lovers!
Was the light they floated in
lamplight, they asked each other,
or light beneath the skin?

And when they looked away,
leaving them for that night
wrapped in each other, they
glowed with a richer light.

In other rooms each tries,
through other nights, to piece
together widened eyes,
mouth, cheek, into a face

familiar as their own.
But darkness dissolves all —
except their mirror-icon
brilliant on the wall.

The patron saints of lovers — lips
still parted, their eyes bright!
Then each, though separate, sleeps
wrapped in remembered light.

4

Tonight is the night of the blue moon
for which we prayed
from midnight to high noon
so many nights and days.

It rises as we climb six flights
of stairs, radiant with such
voltage that stars and streetlights
blaze if our fingers touch.

The sky is a bell of blue metal
that finds its tongue when we lie down —
the room rocking a little
as the moon swings over the town.

One slow note from the sky's rim
flows into another. The heavens
open and we swim
through mounting seas of resonance —

crest after crest, and the seventh wave
foaming over all.
Blue moon, what a tide moves when you move!
What seabed shall contain it should it fall?

5

After the moth's kiss
and the bee's,
but not in a gondola, this
matched by no metaphor
but that reflection of itself,
the kiss that seals my groin to yours.

6

Why such drooping plumage
and so empty-throated
when I set you free?
And yet you lift your head
and sing and sing for me
when covered in her cage.

7

Waking, I caught the world off-balance,
I will not say off-true
for it has not righted since
my eyes opened to you

turning to me. To live
in our bodies till now
and never know them! We leave
a tilting bed knowing we know.

Love is yeast. My thoughts rise
level with God's, as high
white clouds remembering
you in a cornflower sky.

All roads this morning
run downhill, shining,
and I round every corner
with the sun in my eyes.

DISABLED SERVICEMAN
with a chestful of gongs
beating time on your mac
to the honky-tonk songs

your accordeon plays,
what made you turn and blaze
at me that song of all songs
today of all days?

My heart between your hands —
blown from its body —
contracts and expands
with the song she sung me,

which your accordeon,
transplanted, pumps through
my veins. Here's money, magician.
And a new song, love, for you.

AFTER 'LA DESSERTE'

Thank you, Matisse,
for the wide-hipped carafe
   you gave me this
   morning, half-

full of the red.
Ever since then it has
   blessed our bed
   with wine-dark light as

we lay loving.
And like pearl divers there
   sometimes coming
   up for air,

we drank a toast
or two or three to things
   lovers prize most —
   till evening brings

the question, how
can this carafe and heart
   be fuller now
   than at the start?

POUR COMMENCER

Take 1 green pepper and 2 tomatoes
and cut them into rings and hearts. Mix those
with olives, black olives, and go for a swim
in a green sea with her (or him).
Then serve your salad on two bellies. Pour
a little sun-warmed olive oil in your
salt navel, some vinegar in hers
(or his), and eat slowly with your fingers.
Empty the bottle. Open a second. Then
lick your plates. You will need them again.

SO MUCH IN COMMON

So much in common being not enough
we move on together, moving back
together down the shadowed tracks
that brought us, singly, under the one roof.

Under the sheet you take me by the hand
to meet a boy among the dunes
who calls you beautiful. I stand
in his footprints to kiss you, brushing the down

along your cheekbone with a salty tongue.
Help me to push the dinghy out.
She gybes again! You seize my coat
with my mother's hand when it was young

as yours, and capsized we jog together —
fingers stiff on the clinkered hull —
hour by numbing hour, until
trawlermen's hands haul us in, to slither

on a deck among mackerel. Slept that night
in a bristling blanket. Blinked
awake, dressed, knowing by instinct
that you too were dressing by mushroom light.

Our fingers meet on your father's landing,
tighten at the treacherous stair,
and we ride on a banister
into an orchard with its branches bending.

That log-stacked summerhouse at the wood's edge
stands on a frontier, where I stood
hearing a foreign language in my blood,
and swung an axe and hammered wedge

after wedge into oozing apple grain.
'How dark it is.' Give me your hand. .
I'll tread the nettles down and bend
the brambles back. If we are lost again

we are lost together. But the dark is pricked
by a star, and the trees draw back
into shadowy rows as the track
turns to an avenue. We correct

our course by the star. And the star grows
to a planet, a window, a room
with a pressure lamp in full bloom
beside the bed. Breathless among pillows

we move on together. Our lungs
increase the flame till its bowl brims
over. The bed's alight, our limbs
blaze through the sheet! We have the gift of tongues,

speaking each other's language not with the mouth
only, but with bodies dumb
before. Now candid, they become
transfigured with the eloquence of truth.

THE SOURCE

*'The dead living in their memories
are, I am persuaded, the source
of all that we call instinct.'*
                    W.B. Yeats

Taking me into your body
you take me out of my own,
releasing an energy,
a spirit, not mine alone

but theirs locked in my cells.
One generation after
another, the blood rose and fell
that lifts us together.

Such ancient, undiminished
longings — my longing! Such
tenderness, such famished
desires! My fathers in search

of fulfilment storm through
my body, releasing now
loved women locked in you
and hungering to be found.

A QUESTION OF FORM AND CONTENT

I owe you an apology,
love my love, for here you are
in a school anthology
without so much as a bra
between your satin self and those
who come upon us in crisp sheets.
What they will make of us, God knows,
but no harm's done if it's
what we make of each other. Let
them observe, love, our *enjambement*.
They shall be guests at the secret
wedding of form and content.

BREAKFAST IN BED

Lying in late:
two croissants, warm
in each other's arms,
on a dazzling plate.

PERSONAL COLUMN

A GOLD LOCKET lost in the street
sometime between heartbeat and heartbeat.
Hinge sealed with the salt from two bodies
whose likeness neither side now carries.
Reward offered: happiness such
as the locket saw from its niche
bless whoever returns it. But
whoever finds and will not part
with it, may the miniature last
night mirrored in his heart be lost
today and found in another heart.

A PAIR OF GOLD DOLPHINS

At sundown, two dolphins
enter the molten bay . . .
and from some other shore
I have seen those gilded fins
stitching the sea before.

Not Curaçao, black
fins only in Tarquah Bay,
silver the hurdling schools
off Delos. . . . At my back
the burning mountain cools.

Its shadow puts out to sea.
And I suddenly know
that if that racing stain
outstrips my memory
they will never surface again.

Too late, for the killer
fin strikes — but look, they leap clear —
imperishable! A pair
of gold dolphins glitter
in the waves of a woman's hair.

MESSAGE RECEIVED

They come together again,
the luminous swift hand over the slow,
and though the watch-pulse does not quicken
as mine quickens, I know

that in another country
a pulse is answering the morse of mine.
Link by link you turn your bracelet slowly,
transmitting the call-sign

of a charged heart. It comes,
clear as Orion tonight, above
the crickets shrilling in the gums.
Out of the darkness, love,

I have your message always
at this hour: in spirit tenderly,
as once tenderly otherwise,
you are receiving me.

AFRICAN VIOLETS

indigo skies
each with its own full moon
shadow the desk. My eyes
stray from my papers. Soon,
forgetting the flowerseller
and the work I meant to do,
I shall persuade myself
these came from you.

HOMECOMING

At 40,000 feet
the dulled blade glimmers as it goes in
steadily, peeling dark skin
from the world turning under it,

and you throw back bedclothes.
Dazzled, when the plane lands
we converge with our lives in our hands
and the peeled sky sweet in our mouths.

PICNIC

Those daisies know too much!
Seeing that kiss, and now
touching what they touch
ought to have made them bow

their heads. You, pressing her thigh —
because you dared to look
your rival in the eye —
shall be pressed in a book.

THE PLAY OF HANDS

'I am the capital', head says,
'and what I say goes
for the barbarous provinces,
fingers and toes —'

as, at the frontier, a thumb
enters the tender groove
between index finger and thumb;
and though your fingers move

with a moth's tact in my hand,
the fire they kindle vaults
from province into province
and the capital melts.

WILLOW-PATTERN BLUES

The willows are gold again
that have been black that have been green,
and I am back where I have been
with the willow-pattern blues
on a juke-box brain.

Down where the willows comb
their hair and a bridge makes mouths in the stream
we walk in a willow-pattern dream;
at midday kicking off shoes
where the grass whispers welcome,

and an emerald thread
shuttles downstream and back. 'We should live
like the kingfishers, love,
and never lose
today's lustre', you said.

And still, however unwise
or unlucky we seem, the kingfisher weaves
between leaves and reflected leaves
in a world contracted to
your willow-pattern eyes.

THROUGH A GLASS

Mid-day, mid-summer
in the middle of England.
The sun on my shoulder,
a glass chill in my hand
lifting to touch lips
with your chill glass. 'To us.'
As the lager lens tips
your face into focus,
it shows you distant, blonde
as the willow behind
you, blonde as the barley
across the lager-bright
river. What can there be
for us but sunlight,
sunlight, sunlight beyond
the chill glass in my hand?

HOPS

After Pasternak

Beneath the willow wound round with ivy
we take cover from the worst
of the storm, with a greatcoat round
our shoulders and my hands around your waist.

I've got it wrong. That isn't ivy
entwined in the bushes round
the wood, but hops. You intoxicate me!
Let's spread the greatcoat on the ground.

A DINNER OF HERBS
with Natalia Volokhova

I

A man in his shirtsleeves,
in front of a window brushed
by restless, importunate leaves,

is translating words put to a stove
or a hissing lamp or the wall
by a man translating his love

into Russian syllables.
In the mouth of the shirtsleeved man
roll words as cold as pebbles

with no more life of their own
than moves in the mouth of the Russian
under his lettered stone . . .

II

You enter the room with a tray
and, when I savour the rich steam
rising from your casserole, say:

'A dinner of herbs where love is.'
I relearn at your hands,
as deftly they fill the dishes,

a lesson learnt long ago.
Sitting cross-legged on the floor
we talk of Shakhmatovo

until the lamp gives up its ghost.
Your head sinks to my shoulder.
And with leaves whitening into frost

against a trembling window,
we make love by stovelight
to the sound of snow.

34

THE LAST WORD

Words, words, you and your damn
words! she said and went out
like a whirlwind, slam-
ming the door.
                    I was about
to say: that without words,
my love, where should we be
today? And afterwards,
stripped to our names and two
cold dates, where shall we be
but in these words for what
we touch and are and do?

IN THE ZOOLOGICAL SECTION

We stop in front of the case
containing skulls of two roe deer
who brought each other to this place.

Their antlers interlocked, they lie
eye-socket to eye-socket
as, starving, they lay eye to eye;

breath mingling as the hours pass,
eyes clouding over, like our own
reflected in the cabinet glass.

AGAIN

I have been there again, and seen the backs
convulsing at the heart of the bazaar,
spasmed with laughter and the lunging jar
of shoulders as the fruit is thrown. A crack

in the crowd wall brought me to the ring
where, linked so one at first could not tell which
was which, the pie-dog and his trembling bitch
suffered the tribesmen's pitiless pelting.

Though terrible their straining from each other,
her crying and his scabbed flanks shaken
with hurt and terror — worse to waken
from that harsh sobbing to the bed's shudder.

THE BEGINNING OF THE END

1

Passing the great plane tree in the square —
and noticing me noticing
the railing's sawn-off arrowhead
ingrown too many rings deep there
in 1940 to be shifted —
you ask me what I am thinking,
and wish the words unsaid.

2

'Our' café
         since a morning
      not to be talked about
      these mornings
                  has put out
its tulip awning,
and the bell above the door
like a clockwork canary
sings its one song.
               As we
   crossed this chequerboard floor

'Buon giorno'
            affable
      as if we were regulars.
      Setting down our saucers
      on the glass-topped table

'Due grandi neri —
this morning, please,
you are my guests. The lease
finito. I shall be
with the vino rosso
next month in Tuscany.
No more grandi neri,
no more espresso.'

Spilt coffee
            spelt my name
      and your name, linked, on this
      glass table — our knees kiss-
      ing under it.
                  The same
finger writes TUSCANY
and rubs it out. We have
run out of words
                  like love.
Next month where shall we be?

3

Getting up to go.
'My gloves!' Floor, seat,
handbag — 'oh no, no,
not in the street!'

      My first present. It
      seemed right and proper
      enough. 'A perfect fit'
      said the girl in the shop
      as one hand pushed
      the other, finger by
      finger, home; and you blushed
      to meet my eye.

Stripped of their shadows,
disconsolate hands stare
at each other and those
inert elsewhere —
the warmth and scent
of their fingers failing,
trampled on the pavement,
impaled on a railing.

MAKING AN END

We call them ours, the leaves we saw —
hand in hand on our daily walk —
bud and break out across the park.

> *If kisses were leaves, we*
> *could cover that tree.*

We could hang every twig — and more,
every twig in the avenue —
with a tear spilt since. But have to
do something else: the hardest thing.
After so much, sharing so much,

> *those ducks in their patch*
> *of daffodils making*
> *love, last year,*

nothing is harder
than making an end.

> *Their love-talk*
> *followed us on our walk*

where today a man on a ladder
is cutting a branch from a tree.
His power-saw snarls as its teeth
take hold, and we underneath
can hear not a word but only
the snarl and the snarling echo.
This is the gate. We have to go
through.

Think how we entered
it first!

The man raises his saw
as if acknowledging us or
waving goodbye (the unspeakable word).
There are no words. And there must be
no looking back. Ten paces, twenty.
Like duellists we turn. Your mouth seems
to be open, black. Your right hand
flutters. The saw screams.

APOLLINAIRE TREPANNED

remembers the red
poem hot from his head
in the palm of his hand.

As rubber gloves
lifted my lid
with my helmet, did
an uprush of doves

flutter the nurses? When
will the birds that filled
my green branches build
there again?

BURNING THE STUBBLE

Another harvest gathered in
worse than the last; only a bin
of rotten grain for all our trouble.
But there is a time for the plough,
a time for harvesting, and now
a time for burning the stubble.

Flames snap at the wind, and it
etches the eye with a bitter
mirage of summer. Returning
I looked for the dip in the ground,
the nest, the unfurled poppy; found
nothing but stubble burning,

~~and~~ charred ground hardening towards frost.
Fire before ice; and the ground must
be ploughed after burning the stubble,
the ground must be broken again.
There can be no new grain
without, first, burning the stubble.

IN THE PARK

Hugging his dolphin, our stone boy stands
snared in his fountain's frozen bowl.
The trees overhead are holding hands   '

two by two to the avenue's ends;
the hand in my pocket worries a hole.
Hugging his dolphin, our stone boy stands

with eyes for nothing but his friend's
blunt head. Why should he care that, bole to bole,
the trees overhead are holding hands

when yours and mine are in different lands
and remembered fingers worry a hole
in my heart? Our stone boy stands

hugging his dolphin as night descends
slashing my face with a wind from the Pole.
The trees overhead are holding hands

and talking in low voices. Mine pretends
there's nothing to say but that, in his bowl,
hugging his dolphin our stone boy stands;
the trees overhead are holding hands.

RESURRECTION

At midday the tree
in the garden throws
a net over me.

Restrained by shadows
as if, while I lay
at its foot, roots rose

and closed over me,
I can feel only
the pulse of the tree.

It draws up, steady
as mercury
from my dark body,

columns of clear
sap. Distilled to this,
I could lie here

forever, putting
my heart into
building and rigging

a beech trunk to climb
every year at this
leafmaking time.

And every year
under me singing,
swinging, I should hear

children whose fathers
call to them nightly
moving among the stars.

THE WRITING ON THE WALL

Open the window, let in the wind
to the room where the stencilled crate
and trunks with our dead selves coffined
in them dark hour by dark hour wait
for morning and the carrier's men.
Give them a sailing wind, and let
it sweep out the bad dreams, broken
dreams, memories we would forget.

At midnight last night wind and moon
were up together, and the tall
acacia at the wind's dictation
scribbled in shadow on that wall
writing I could not read; then struck
it out and wrote again. I've been
awake since, trying to break
its code, but now the wall's wiped clean.

Throw all the windows open. Here
it comes, the breath of the dead
smelling of garlic and stale beer
and smoke. And blowing us good
or ill? I could almost believe
in a change of tune, a new note
this morning as we leave
for wherever, whatever the wind wrote.

MOTHER AND CHILD

Lighter by a life, you settle back
into a dune of pillows;
remembering, as the tide runs slack,
its current the night it rose
wrestling through you, lifting inland
the unknown here, at the tide's return,
made known, breathing under your hand.

Black grapes, as long in the growing, torn
from shrunk capillaries of the vine,
bleed in your mouth, letting the rain
sucked by the sun from the raw earth
run back into the earth again.

AT BEDTIME

Reading you the story you cannot understand
any more than another, before the light
goes out, I am distracted by the hand
turning the page too early or too late —

as I was in the bookshop, hearing today
that other father with the small son say:
'We need a book. What would you recommend
for a four-year-old starting to read?'

And a dam in my head broke under the thought
of things your simple hand would never make:
toys, love, and poems scattering the comfort
of commandments you can never break.

THE ALMOND TREE REVISITED

He looks up, wondering why
we've stopped, to see a pink cloud cross
the untroubled blue of his eye.

And not knowing how it was
seven years back, he tugs me on.
When I was acquainted with loss

you blessed me with a vision
of blossom welling from dark veins.
Today, with my light-headed son,

I stand in your shadow again
troubled with loss: the loss of power,
not his, but mine, the poet's an-

cient power of giving praise and honour:
in gratitude, blessing a tree
above its kind with a continual flower.

THIS MORNING

The weathercock once again heading south
catches the sun's eye, and my daughter says
the blackbird has a crocus in its mouth.

'Spring's here',
                    I tell her.
                                 'Here for always?'
'No, but for now.'
                          'Now is for always,
now is for always',
                          she sings, as she takes
my hand and we take each other to school.

'I'll pick you some flowers and I'll make you cakes
and I'll swing in the sun all afternoon.'

And I'll spend half the night with a worn pen
in that worn hand you're holding, one half-moon
eclipsed by a bruise, writing again
something I cannot say: that now is not
forever and to have is not to hold,
but they, you will learn, have nothing, that
have nothing to lose. Your fingers unfold
their first, delicate leaves. Among them, may
the bird in your hand set your veins singing
from moment to moment, always,
as mine do this morning.